PROGRAM NOTES

“Tapestry of Light” is a joining of traditional carols, primarily from the British Isles, with scripture reading and candle lighting. I was inspired by recent trips to Ireland, Scotland, Wales and England to create a work that celebrates the rich heritage of seasonal song that is part of this great tradition.

The suggestions indicated in the book are merely templates for you to use as you design your service. Please insert your own holiday traditions when using this work. In providing two different voicing and orchestral options, I hoped to enable choirs of any size to present this work. The inclusion of visual elements and choreography options (Digital Resource Kit) are all optional and are provided as a guide for directors who seek to make their cantata presentations even more creative.

THE LIGHT OF CREATION

NARRATOR 1: *[From off stage in darkness.]*

In the beginning God created the heavens and the earth. The earth was formless and empty. Darkness was over the surface of the deep, and the Spirit of God was hovering over the waters. And God said, "Let there be light," and there was light. *(Gen. 1:1-3 NIV)*

[Raise the lights and light the first candle(s).]

CAROLS OF HOPE AND LIGHT

Words by
JOSEPH M. MARTIN (BMI)

Based on tunes:
I SAW THREE SHIPS
SUSSEX CAROL
IN DULCI JUBILO
Arranged by
JOSEPH M. MARTIN (BMI)

* Tune: I SAW THREE SHIPS, Traditional English Carol

30
3
mf
Re -
mf
30
mp
33
joice, re-joice, pre - pare the way for Christ - mas day, for Christ-mas day. Re -
33
mf (Accompanist may double voices if desired.)
37
joice, re-joice, de - clare your praise on Christ - mas day in the morn -
37
mf

41
ing.
41
mp
45
4
45
49
* mp unis.
A - rise and shine! Your Light _ will come, and
p
Al - le - lu - ia! Oo
49
p

53
God will send His cho - sen one. A - rise and shine! Your
mp
Oo
Rise and shine! Your
53
mp
56
mf
Light will come. Re - joice and see what the Lord has done.
mf
Light will come.
56
mf
59
60
mp
Come raise your songs of joy and
mp
59
60
mp

* Tune: IN DULCI JUBILO, Traditional German Carol

74
voice. Give ye heed to what we say:
mp
77
mf
"News! News! Soon the Lord will come to stay.
80
To a low - ly cat - tle stall, God will give a

83
gift to all." Lift a song of praise!
86
Lift a song of praise!
f
90
6
92
mf
Al - le - lu - ia!
ff

94
f unis.
Sing to God a ju - bi - lant song! Re -
f
94
97
joice, re-joice, your Light will come on Christ - mas day, on Christ - mas day. Re -
97
f
101
joice, re - joice, your light will come on Christ - mas day in the
101

104
7
106
driving to the end
morn - ing!
Let all the peo - ple
Re -
driving to the end
107
sing!
Let stee - ples ring,
for on
joice, give thanks and sing!
Let stee - ples ring,
110
cresc.
ff
Christ - mas day,
Light will come!
for on Christ - mas day,
Light will come!

THE LIGHT OF PREPARATION

NARRATOR 1:

The voice of one crying in the wilderness: "Prepare the way of the LORD. Make straight in the desert a highway for our God. Every valley shall be exalted; and every mountain and hill brought low. The crooked places shall be made straight; and the rough places smooth. The glory of the LORD shall be revealed; and all flesh shall see it together; for the mouth of the LORD has spoken." *(Isaiah 40:3-5)*

NARRATOR 2:

I, the LORD, have called you in righteousness. I will take hold of your hand. I will keep you and will make you to be a covenant for the people and a light for the Gentiles. *(Isaiah 42:6)*

LONGING FOR THE LIGHT

Words by
JOSEPH M. MARTIN (BMI)

Based on tunes:
SCARBOROUGH FAIR
GREENSLEEVES
Arranged by
JOSEPH M. MARTIN (BMI)

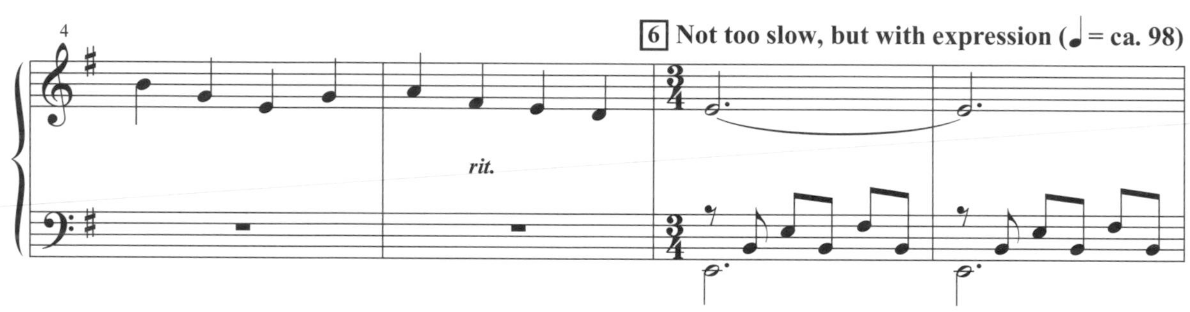

* Tune: VENI EMMANUEL, Plainsong
** Tune: SCARBOROUGH FAIR, Traditional English Melody

12
mp
Come and ran - som Is - ra -
mp
16
18
el.
Come with pow'r and
20
p
maj - es - ty.
Loose our
p
24
9
bonds and set us free.

28
mp
Come, come Thou Wis - dom
MALE SOLO
mp
Come, Thou Wis - dom from on high.
28
mp
32
from on high. Come and bring Your guid - ing
Come and bring Your guid - ing
32
36
38 mf
light. Guide us with Thy
mf
light. Guide us with Thy
36
38
mf

* Tune: GREENSLEEVES, Traditional English Melody

48
joice, re - joice! Em - man - u - el shall
48
f
52
come to thee, O Is - ra - el. Re -
52
56
dim. poco a poco
joice, re - joice! The Light will come, the
dim. poco a poco
56
dim. poco a poco

60
mf
Babe, the Son of Ma - ry.
mf
60
mf
64
11
66
Come, O come, great
64
66
68
Lord of grace. Come, in - hab - it all of our
68

73
75
praise.
Fill us with Your
77
unis.
peace and light;
death's dark shad - ows
81
84
put to flight.
Re - joice, re -
f
3

85
joice! Em - man - u - el shall come to
85
89
12
92
thee, O Is - ra - el. Re - joice, re -
89
92
93
dim. poco a poco
joice! The Light will come, the Babe, the
dim. poco a poco
93
dim. poco a poco

97
mp
13
Son of Ma - ry.
mp
97
mp

102
FEMALE SOLO
p
rit.
Come, O come, Em - man - u - el,
p
rit.

107
Slowly (♩ = ca. 72)
Em - man - u - el.

THE LIGHT OF ANTICIPATION

NARRATOR 1:

Hear this promise from scripture:

The desert and the parched land will be glad.
  The wilderness will rejoice and blossom.
Like the crocus, it will burst into bloom.
  It will rejoice greatly and shout for joy.
All will see the glory of the LORD,
  and the splendor of our God. *(Isaiah 35:1-2)*

[Light the next candle(s).]

AN ADVENT GARDEN

Words by
JOSEPH M. MARTIN (BMI)

Tune: **BROTHER JAMES' AIR**
by J. L. MACBETH BAIN (1860-1925)
Arranged by
JOSEPH M. MARTIN (BMI)

13
mp
15
The gift of love sent from a - bove will
grace - ful winds will blow.
13
15
17
15
like a gar - den grow.
17
mp
21
mp
22
The des - ert sands will come a - live as streams be - gin to
mp
21
22

25
flow. The bar - ren lands will bloom and thrive. The hills will be made
25
29
p unis.
low. In ev-'ry place, God's gift of grace will like a gar - den
p
29
p
33
16
mp
mf
35
grow. Al - le - lu - ia! Al - le - lu - ia! Let the
mp
mf
33
35
mp
mf

37
earth lift its voice; for a new rose is bloom - ing in
41
Zi - on. Let the gar - den re - joice.
45
17
rit.
f unis.
The
f
rit.

48
a tempo
with confidence
li - on and the lamb will rest. The bear will feed on straw. In
48
a tempo
with confidence
f
52
Zi - on hope will reign at last. A Child will lead them all.
52
56
mf
57
The gift of peace will be re-leased and like a gar - den
mf
56
57
mf

60
rit.
mp
grow.
Then
mp
60
mp
rit.
64
Slower
peace, like a gar - den, will grow.
64
Slower
p
68
rit.
68
rit.
pp

THE LIGHT OF THE ANNUNCIATION

NARRATOR 2:

Hear the words of the Prophet:

Therefore, the Lord Himself will give you a sign: the virgin will be with Child and will give birth to a Son, and will call Him Immanuel. *(Isaiah 7:14)*

Now hear words form the gospel of Luke:

God sent the angel Gabriel to Nazareth, a town in Galilee, to a virgin pledged to be married to a man named Joseph, a descendant of David. The virgin's name was Mary. The angel went to her and said, "Greetings, you who are highly favored, the Lord is with you."

Mary was greatly troubled at his words and wondered what kind of greeting this might be. But the angel said to her, "Do not be afraid, Mary. You have found favor with God. You will conceive and give birth to a Son, and you are to call Him Jesus. He will be great, and He will be called the Son of the Most High. The Lord God will give Him the throne of His father David, and He will reign over Jacob's descendants forever. His kingdom will never end." *(Luke 1:26-33)*

THE HOLY CHILD OF MARY

Words by
JOSEPH M. MARTIN (BMI)

Based on tunes:
THE HOLLY AND THE IVY
SANS DAY CAROL
Arranged by
JOSEPH M. MARTIN (BMI))

Gracefully (♩ = ca. 120)

* Tune: THE HOLLY AND THE IVY, Traditional English melody

12
peace and love sent from a - bove. You are wor-thy of our praise.
tr
16 BARITONE
mp
19
The stars that shine in
20
heav - en, the snow up - on the trees are pure and bright and
24
filled with light, but none com-pares with Thee.
legato

* Tune: SANS DAY CAROL, Traditional English melody

40
won - der of heav - en has come to our night.
legato
44
mf unis.
46
The Son born of Ma - ry is
mf
48
p
mp
mf
God's per - fect light. No - el, no - el. The

52
55
Son born of Ma - ry is God's per - fect light.
mf
56
cresc. poco a poco
60
64
SOPRANO
ALTO
BARITONE
20
allargando
f
67
a tempo
with great rejoicing
O ho - ly night of

68
wonders, O night when Christ came down, let the earth rejoice with
68
72
tune-ful noise and a ju-bi-la-tion sound. Al-le-lu-ia! Al-le-
75
72
75
76
lu-ia! Al-le-lu-ia! Al-le-lu-ia! Re-joice! Al-le-
76

lu - ia! Al - le - lu - ia! Christ is born!
ff
84
Al - le - lu - ia! Christ is
cresc.
born!
Re - joice!

THE LIGHT OF INCARNATION

NARRATOR 2:

For unto us a Child is born. Unto us a Son is given; and the government shall be upon His shoulder; and His name shall be called Wonderful, Counselor, the Mighty God, the Everlasting Father, the Prince of Peace. *(Isaiah 9:6)*

NARRATOR 1:

In those days Caesar Augustus issued a decree that a census should be taken of the entire Roman world. So Joseph also went up from the town of Nazareth in Galilee to Judea, to Bethlehem, the town of David, because he belonged to the house and line of David. He went there to register with Mary, who was pledged to be married to him and was expecting a child. While they were there, the time came for the Baby to be born, and she gave birth to her firstborn - a Son. She wrapped Him in cloths and placed Him in a manger, because there was no guest room available for them. *(Luke 2:1-7)*

[Light the next candle(s).]

O WONDROUS NIGHT

Words by
JOSEPH M. MARTIN (BMI)

Tune: **LONDONDERRY AIR**
Traditional Irish Tune
Arranged by
JOSEPH M. MARTIN (BMI)

9
sight, the an - gel choirs are wing - ing, bring - ing the
O glo - rious sight,___ an - gels are bring - ing
9
11
news of peace to all the earth. Re - joice! Re -
good news of peace to all the earth.
11
13
joice! This is a time for wor - ship! Lift up your
13

voice and tune your heart for praise. O won-drous
night that brought the gift of Je - sus.
O won-drous night that saw the light of grace.
dim.
rit.
a tempo
a tempo
rit.

22
22
22
mp
f
dim.

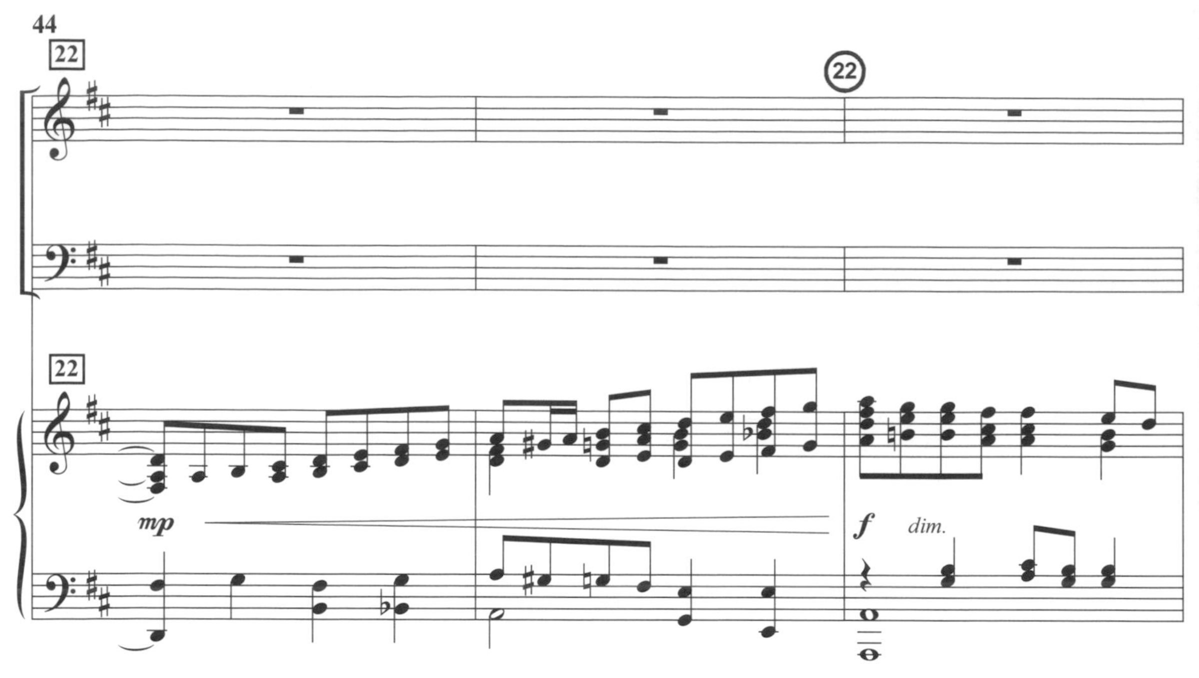

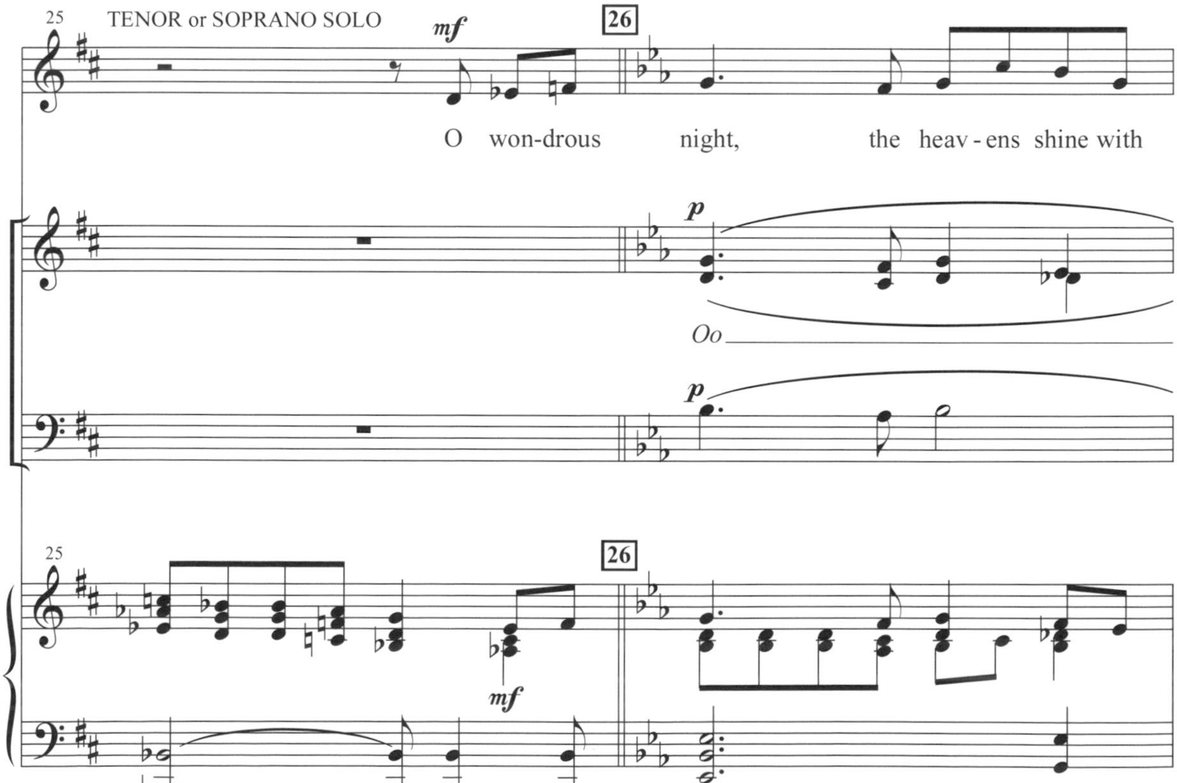
25
TENOR or SOPRANO SOLO
mf
26
O won-drous night, the heav-ens shine with
p
Oo
p
25
26
mf

27
glo - ry, beam - ing with light, love paints the shad - ows
27
29
gold; and from the heights, the an - gels share the
mp
p
The shad - ows gold.
Oo
mp
p
Oo
29

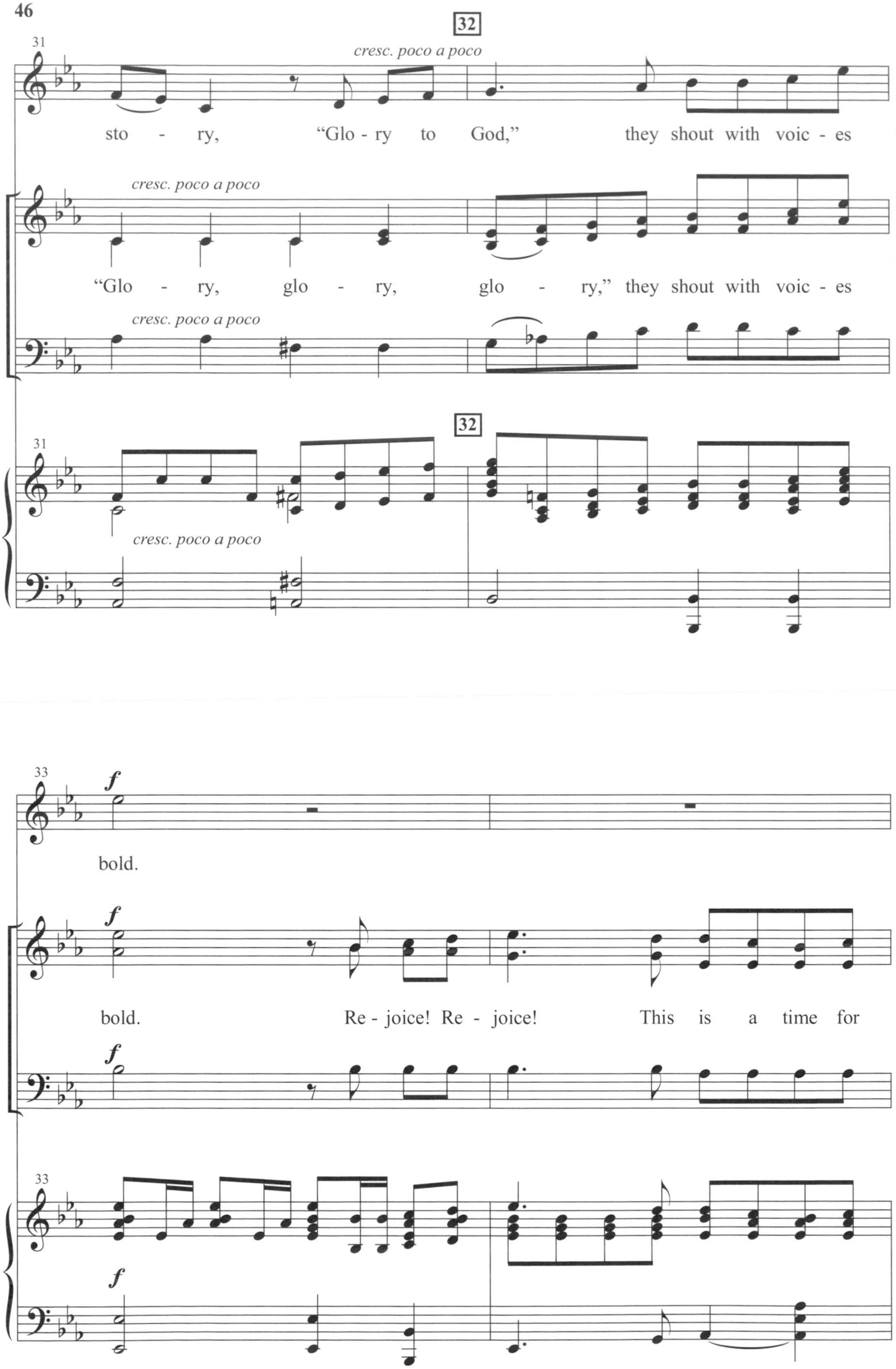

33
f
bold.

f
bold. Re - joice! Re - joice! This is a time for

f

33

f

35
wor - ship! Lift up your voice and tune your heart for
35
37
praise. O won-drous night that brought the gift of
ff
ff
37
ff

39
rit.
Slower
mf
41
O won-drous night that saw the
Je - sus.
O won-drous night that saw the
mf
mf
39
Slower
41
rit.
mf
42
rit.
mp
p
light of grace.
rit.
mp
p
light of grace.
mp
p
42
rit.
mp
p

THE LIGHT OF DECLARATION

NARRATOR 2:

There were shepherds living out in the fields nearby, keeping watch over their flocks at night. An angel of the Lord appeared to them and the glory of the Lord shone around them. They were terrified!

But the angels said to them, “Do not be afraid, for I bring you good news of great joy that will be for all the people. Today, in the town of David, a Savior has been born to you. He is Christ the Lord. This will be a sign to you: you will find a Baby wrapped in cloths, lying in a manger.”

And suddenly, a great company of the heavenly hosts appeared with the angel, praising God and saying, “Glory to God in the highest and on earth peace to all people on whom His favor rests.” *(Luke 2:8-14)*

[Light the next candle(s).]

A CELTIC NOEL

Words by
MICHAEL BARRETT *and*
JOSEPH M. MARTIN (BMI)

Based on tunes:
CANDLER
FOREST GREEN
Arranged by
MICHAEL BARRETT (BMI)
and JOSEPH M. MARTIN (BMI)

* Tune: FOREST GREEN, Traditional English Melody
** Tune: CANDLER, Traditional Scottish Melody

13
a - tion is sing - ing as an - gels take wing.
BARITONE
mf
No - el, no - el! Let
13
16
great ju - bi - la - tion re - sound through cre - a - tion to
16
18
f
20
Sing al - le - lu - ia,
f
wel-come the King.
18
20
f

21
al - le - lu - ia! Glo - ri - a, glo - ri - a!
23
unis.
Glo - ry to God! No - el, no - el! The
25
song is be - gin - ning with praise and thanks - giv - ing. Sing

"Je - sus is born."
mf
No -
mp
No - el, sing we no -
el, no - el! The an - gels are prais - ing. The
mf
el!
Sing we no -
shep - herds are rais - ing their voice to the sky. No -

33
unis.
el, no - el! Come
el, no - el! Lay gifts now be - fore Him. Come
33
35
f
kneel and a - dore Him, the Sav - ior di - vine. Sing
f
35
3
38
al - le - lu - ia, al - le - lu - ia! Glo - ri - a, glo - ri - a!
38
f

41
unis.
Glo - ry to God.
No - el, no - el! God's
41
43
light is up - on us. His Word is a - mong us, for
43
45
46
Je - sus is born.
45
46
mf

* Words: Edmund H. Sears (1810-1876), alt.

60
mf
61
"Peace on the earth, good will to all, from
mf
gold: "Peace on earth, good will to all, from
60
61
mf
63
heav'n's all-grac-ious King." The world in so - lemn
63
66
cresc. poco a poco
still - ness lay, to hear the glo - ri - ous
cresc. poco a poco
66
cresc. poco a poco

68
26
an - gels sing! Sing No - el! No -
No -
70
el, no - el! The heav-ens are ring-ing. Cre - a - tion is sing-ing as
el, no - el, no - el!
73
unis.
an-gels take wing. No - el, no - el! Re -
An-gels take wing. No - el no - el! Let great ju - bi - la - tion re -

76
sound through cre - a - tion to wel-come the King. Sing
sound through cre - a - tion to wel-come the King.
76
78
al - le-lu - ia, al - le-lu - ia! Glo-ri - a, glo-ri - a!
78
81
unis.
Glo - ry to God! No - el, no - el! The
81

83
mf
cresc. poco a poco
song is be - gin - ning with praise and thanks - giv - ing. Sing glo - ri - a, glo - ri - a,
86
f
glo - ri - a! Glo - ry to God! Sing no -
89
ff
el! Sing no - el! Sing no - el!

THE LIGHT OF REVELATION

NARRATOR I:

Arise, shine, for your light has come,
and the glory of the LORD rises upon you.
See, darkness covers the earth
and thick darkness is over the peoples,
but the LORD rises upon you
and His glory appears over you.
Nations will come to your light,
and the kings to the brightness of your dawn.
(Isaiah 60:1-3)

NARRATOR 2:

After Jesus was born in Bethlehem in Judea, during the time of King Herod, Magi from the east came to Jerusalem and asked, "Where is the one who has been born king of the Jews? We saw His star when it rose and we have come to worship Him." *(Matthew 2:1-2)*

[Light the next candle(s).]

CAROLS OF THE QUEST

Words by
JOSEPH M. MARTIN (BMI)

Based on tunes:
GARTAN
IRBY
KINGSFOLD
DIX
FOREST GREEN

Arranged by
JOSEPH M. MARTIN (BMI)

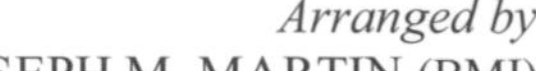

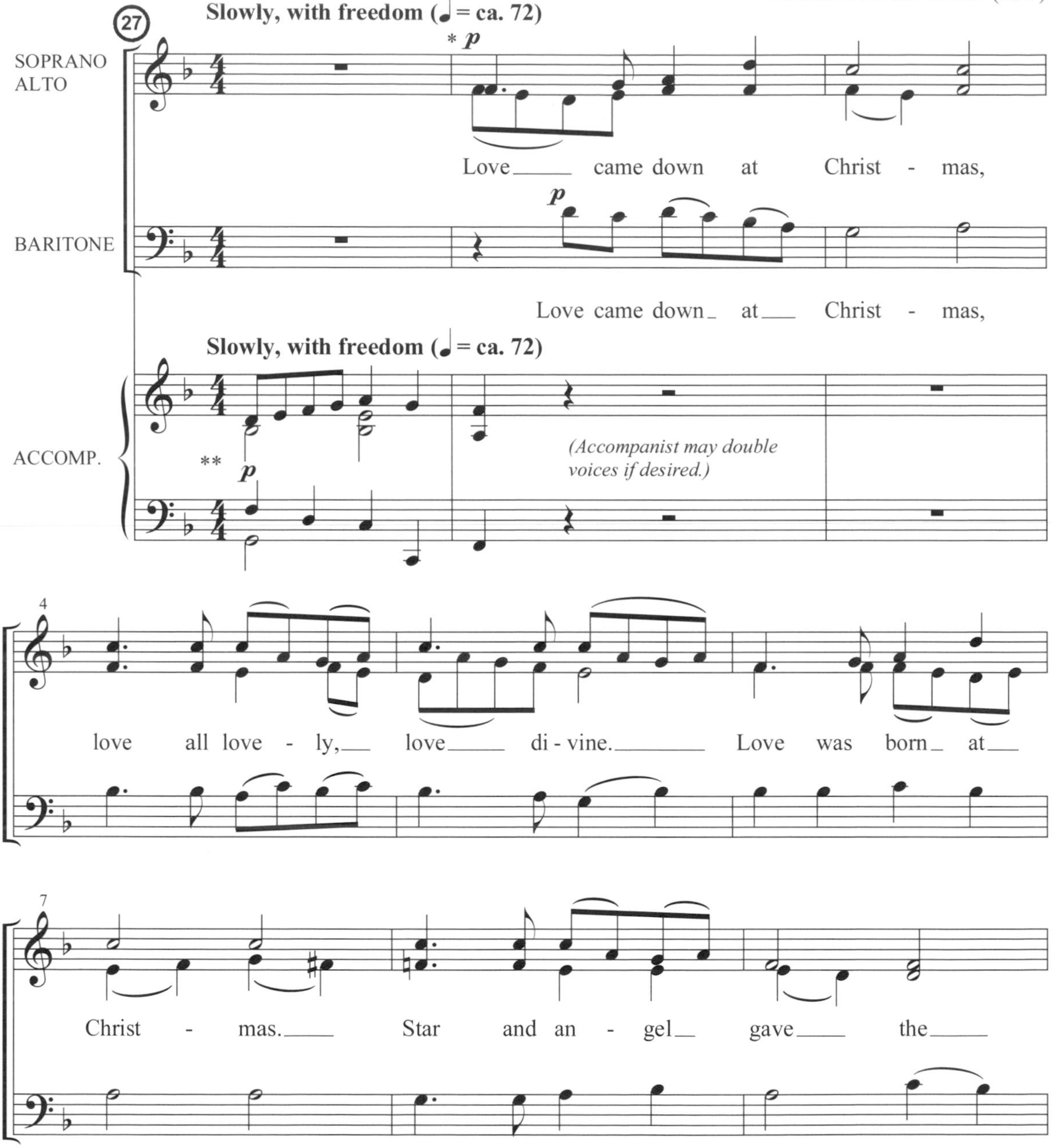
27
Slowly, with freedom (♩ = ca. 72)
SOPRANO
ALTO
* p
Love came down at Christ - mas,
BARITONE
p
Love came down at Christ - mas,
Slowly, with freedom (♩ = ca. 72)
ACCOMP.
**
p
(Accompanist may double voices if desired.)
4
love all love - ly, love di - vine. Love was born at
7
Christ - mas. Star and an - gel gave the

* Tune: GARTAN, Traditional Irish Melody
Words: Christina G. Rossetti, 1830-1894
** Introduction is optional.

* Tune: IRBY, Henry John Gauntlett, 1805-1876
Words: Cecil Frances Alexander, 1818-1895

* Tune: KINGSFOLD, Traditional English Melody
Words: Louis F. Benson, 1855-1930, alt.

29
sing a song of Beth - le - hem, of seek - ers from a -
29
marziale - light and detached
mp
32
far who trav - eled through the wil - der - ness, in -
32
35
spired by heav - en's star. The light that shone on
mf
37
mf
35
37
mf

* Tune: DIX, Conrad Kocher, 1786-1872

* Tune: FOREST GREEN, Traditional English Melody

56
star of won - der, star of might, shine down on us we
56
f
59
f unis.
As with glad - ness, kings of old did the guid - ing
pray.
59
62
star be - hold.
Burn bright your hope - ful mes - sage clear in
62

As with joy they hailed its light,
ev - 'ry heart to - day.
lead - ing on - ward, beam - ing bright.
O
Morn - ing Star, rise in our lives and lead us to Love's

74
unis.
place, and teach us to be stars of light and
77
79
ff
peo - ple of your grace. Make us peo - ple
80
of your grace.

THE LIGHT OF PROCLAMATION

NARRATOR 1:

You are the light of the world. A town built on a hill cannot be hidden. Neither do people light a lamp and put it under a bowl. Instead they put it on its stand, and it gives light to everyone in the house. In the same way, let your light shine before others, that they may see your good deeds and glorify your Father in heaven. *(Matthew 5:14-16)*

[Light the next candle(s).]

A CELTIC GLORIA!

Words by
JOSEPH M. MARTIN (BMI)

Based on tunes:
ASH GROVE
ST. DENIO
Arranged by
JOSEPH M. MARTIN (BMI)

* Tune: ASH GROVE, Welsh melody

13
la - tion sing, "Je - sus is born!"
13
17
19
The stars all are sing - ing. The
(mel.)
17
19
21
bells all are ring - ing. The peo - ple are bring - ing their
21

25 (34) (mel.) *f* [28]

praise_ to the Lord! Sing,_ "Glo -

f

Sing!*(ng)**

25 [28]

f

29

- ri - a! Glo - ri - a! Glo -

Sing! Sing! Sing!

29

33 *mf unis.*

- ri - a! Je - sus is born!" The_

mf

33

* Close immediately to the "ng."

37
mu - sic is swell - ing. The heav - ens are tell - ing with
37
mf
41
44
songs, so com - pell - ing, that "Je - sus is born!"
41
44
45
50
35
mp

* Tune: ST. DENIO, Welsh hymn tune

67
f
- ri - a! Je - sus is born!" Come ce - le - brate
f
67
f
71
joy all you peo - ple of light!
71
75
mf unis.
77
The Sav - ior is born on this
mf
75
77
mf

79
cresc.
glo - rious ho - ly night, on this
cresc.
79
cresc.
83
36
f
86
with great rejoicing
glo - ri - ous night! A new day is
f
83
86
with great rejoicing
f
87
break - ing. A new hope is wak - ing. God's prom - ise is
87

91
94
tak - ing our dark - ness a - way. The day shines with
95
glo - ry as dawn tells the sto - ry, for this is the
with grace.
99
37
morn - ing God wakes us with, wakes us with grace. Sing,
ff

103
"Glo - ri - a! Glo - ri - a!
103
ff
107
Glo - ri - a! Je - sus is
107
110
sfp
born!"
sfp
f unis.
Give
f
110

114
praise all cre - a - tion. Re - joice ev - 'ry__ na - tion. With
114
f
118
glad ju - bi - la - tion sing, "Je - sus is
118
122
ff
born!"
ff
122
ff

THE LIGHT OF CONSECRATION

NARRATOR 1:

Then Jesus spoke to the people, He said, "I am the light of the world, whoever follows me will never walk in darkness, but will have the light of life." *(John 8:12)*

[Light the next candle(s).]

BETHLEHEM LIGHT

Words by
PHILLIPS BROOKS (1835-1893)

Based on tune:
FARE THEE WELL
Traditional Irish Melody
Arranged by
JOSEPH M. MARTIN (BMI)

12
bove thy deep and dream - less sleep, the si - lent stars go
15
mf
16
by. Yet in thy dark street shin - eth the
mf
18
poco rit.
mp
a tempo
ev - er - last - ing Light; and all the hopes and fears of
a tempo
mp
poco rit.
21
all the years are met in thee to - night.

24
39
cresc.

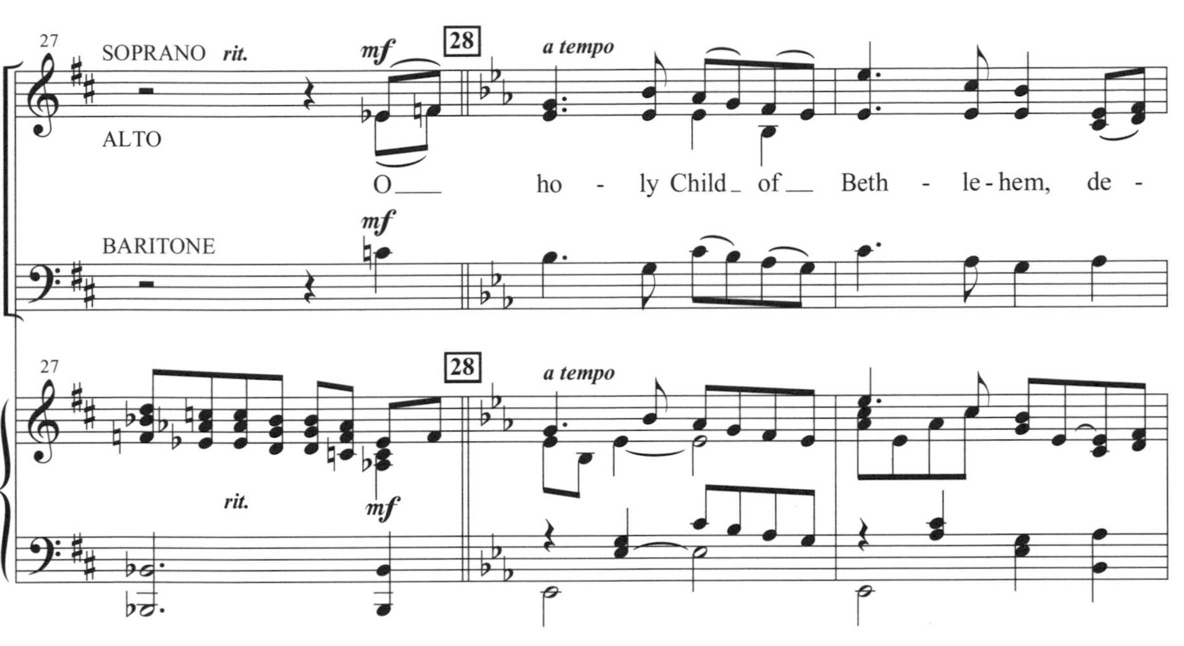
27
SOPRANO rit.
mf
28
a tempo
ALTO
O ho - ly Child of Beth - le - hem, de -
BARITONE
mf
27
28
a tempo
rit.
mf

30
scend on us we pray. Cast out our sin and
30

33
en - ter in. Be born in us to - day. We
f
36
hear the Christ - mas an - gels the
unis.
38
great glad ti - dings tell. O come, O come to us. A -
mf

41
unis.
dim. poco a poco
rit.
bide with us, our Lord, Em - man - u - el.
dim.
Em - man - u -
dim. poco a poco
rit.
44
Slower to the end
SOLO mp
O come to us. A - bide with us, our
el.
44
Slower to the end
mp
47
rit.
p
Lord, Em - man - u - el.
rit.
p

THE LIGHT OF CELEBRATION

NARRATOR I:

In the beginning was the Word, and the Word was with God, and the Word was God. He was with God in the beginning. Through Him all things were made. Without Him nothing was made that has been made. In Him was life, and that life was the light of all people. *(John 1:1-4)*

NARRATOR 2:

Let us therefore rejoice, for God, through Christ, has made us His children of Light. We are now a reflection of His glory. As we forsake the darkness of this world, we freely choose the illumination of God's truth and grace. Let us now shine our light before all people, so that by the light of our love, they may see the glory of God in all we say and do.

[Light the remaining candles.]

CAROLS OF CELEBRATION

Words by
JOSEPH M. MARTIN (BMI)

Based on tunes:
GLOUCESTERSHIRE WASSAIL
WASSAIL SONG
GOD REST YE MERRY GENTLEMEN
IN DULCI JUBILO, I SAW THREE SHIPS
and **ADESTE FIDELES**

Arranged by
JOSEPH M. MARTIN (BMI)

* Tune: GLOUCESTERSHIRE WASSAIL, Traditional English Melody

30
joice, let al - le - lu - ias ring.
A -
34
wake, a - wake for the morn-ing is nigh. Dawn breaks with sing - ing and
37
ev - er - last - ing light, with ev - er - last - ing light. God sent us His Son. Re -

* Tune: WASSAIL SONG, Traditional English Melody

50
mf
grace. Gath - er at the man - ger and bring a gift of
mf
50
mf
54
f
55
praise! Sing for joy! Praise the Lord! Let your
f
54
55
f
57
mu - sic be re - stored! Sing for joy! Tell the
57

* Tune: GOD REST YE MERRY GENTLEMEN, Traditional English Melody
Words: Traditional English

71
to the Lord sing prais - es, all you with - in this
71
74
mp unis.
and with true love and broth - er - hood, each
place;
74
77
mf
oth - er now em - brace; for
mf
77

80
Christ is born in Beth - le - hem and comes to bring us
80
mf
83
grace. O ti - dings of com - fort and of
83
86
unis.
joy, com-fort and joy. O ti - dings of com - fort and of
86

* Tune: IN DULCI JUBILO, Traditional German Melody
Words: Traditional Latin, Tr. John Mason Neale, 1818-1866

* Tune: I SAW THREE SHIPS, Traditional English Melody

* Tune: ADESTE FIDELES, John Francis Wade, 1710-1786
Words: Latin Hymn, John Francis Wade, 1710-1786, Tr. Frederick Oakeley, 1802-1880

122
strong to the end
come let us a - dore Him. O
122
strong to the end
ff
126
come let us a - dore
126
129
130
Him. O come let us a -
129
130

132
dore Him, Christ,
135
driving to the end
the Lord!
Come a -
138
fff
dore Him, Christ, the Lord!